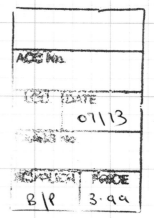

The Usborne book of
Drawing,
doodling
and
colouring
for Girls

Designed and illustrated by
Erica Harrison, Emily Beevers, Non Figg,
Jan McCafferty, Jessica Taunton
and Hannah Davies

Written by Lucy Bowman

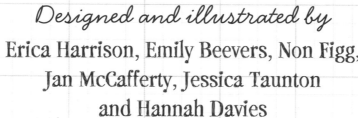

How to use this book...

On some of the pages you'll find ideas for what to do, but you can do whatever you like.

Use pens, pencils or crayons to complete the pictures.

You could fill in large areas, or add stripes, spots or patterns of your own.

When you draw on top of a shape with a pen, wait for a couple of seconds for the ink to dry, so that it doesn't smudge.

Doodle faces and patterns on these owls.

Draw shooting stars
all over the place.

Finish these rows of houses.

Doodle doors, windows and decorations. Who do you think lives inside?

Doodle more caterpillars and tasty leaves.

Munch, munch, munch...

How many greens and yellows do you have? Use them to fill in the forest.

Where are the rest of the dogs?

Give them bones to chew and toys to play with.

Fill the pages with hundreds of circles.

Doodle lots of flowers.

Add some busy bugs, too.

Buzzzzz

It's a sunny day, so fill the washing line with clothes.

Odd socks...

...Make them pairs.

Decorate.

Design.

Customize.

Use your felt pens to finish the outfits.

Red, purple,
green, orange,
yellow, pink...
you choose!

Blonde or
brunette?

Sketch more jumping horses.

These sweet treats have just been baked and decorated.

Cover the pages
with more cupcakes
and cookies.

Fill in the seahorses and seaweed.

Decorate them
with pretty
patterns too.

Build the robots.

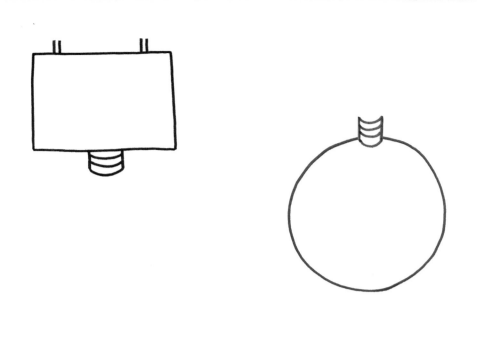

Give them buttons,
dials, lights and wheels.

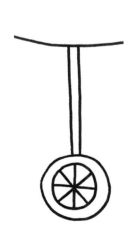

Doodle more eggs and hens.

Decorate the plain eggs.

Fill the pages with supergirls.

Whoosh!

Yummy red strawberries...

Chocolate icing...

Smiling faces...

These masks need decorating with elegant patterns.

Doodle more branches.

Doodle more birds.

Doodle more flowers.

Draw different faces on these animal heads.

Draw more swimming mermaids...

...and bubbles floating in the water.

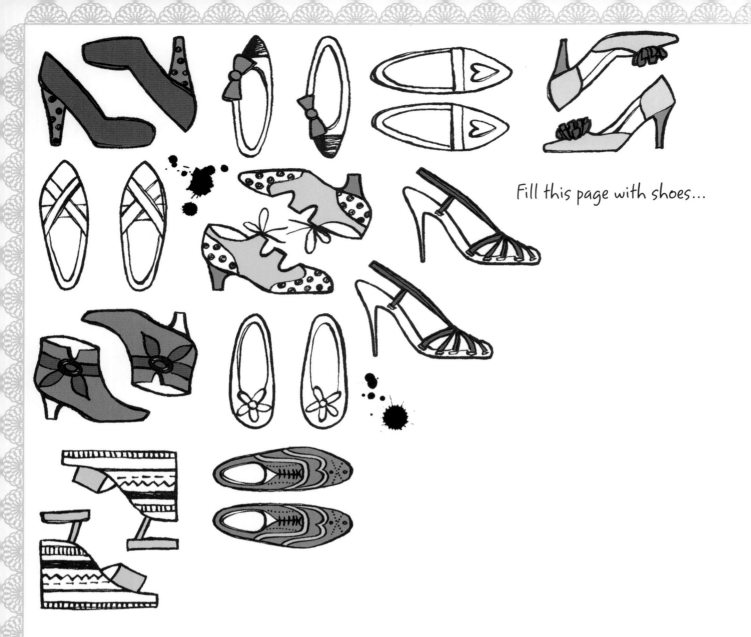

Fill this page with shoes...

...and this page with bags.

Doodle patterns on the flowers.

Give us stripes or spots, bells or bows...

Fill the page with zigzag patterns.

Doodle lots more bright
toadstools sprouting up.

Doodle more flowers and buzzing bees.

Doodle on the dolphins.
Some of the birds might
like patterns too.

Draw fish in the sea.

Add patterns to the waves.

Design the fabric for these dresses.

Add more roses, too.

Finish the tiaras, then doodle more.

Decorate these hearts.

Fill in the ice-cream cones and doodle on yummy toppings.

Fill the pages with patterned bugs.

Doodle patterns on these flamenco dancers' dresses.

Add frills
and flowers
to their hair.

Some of these shells need a snail...

...and some of these snails need a shell.

Doodle more bright shapes.

Roses, roses everywhere...fill the pages with more.

The prince and princess want a bigger castle.
Help them by drawing more walls and turrets.

Decorate the flags.

These tea things
need decorating...

Doodle more hearts across the pages.

Doodle bright patterns on the fish.

Decorate
these gifts.

Draw more flying fairies.

Make them all shades of the rainbow.

Doodle more rainbows, clouds and stars all over these pages.

Doodle black fish swimming in the sea...

...Add some coral and seaweed too.

Use your pens and pencils to finish these houses.

Who lives inside?

Finish these
necklaces.

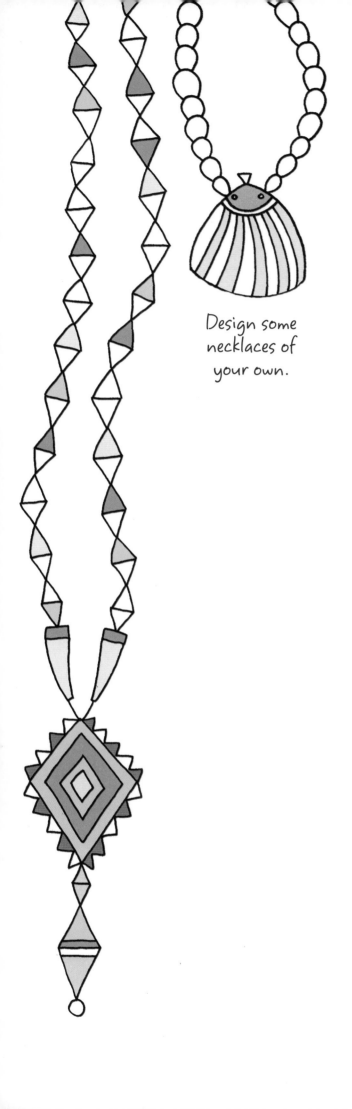

Design some
necklaces of
your own.

Fill in these dancers' dresses with delicate patterns.

Doodle decorations in their hair.

Doodle more fluttering butterflies.

Doodle patterns on these fantastic flamingoes.

Who said they all had to be pink?

Scribble with these pens and pencils...

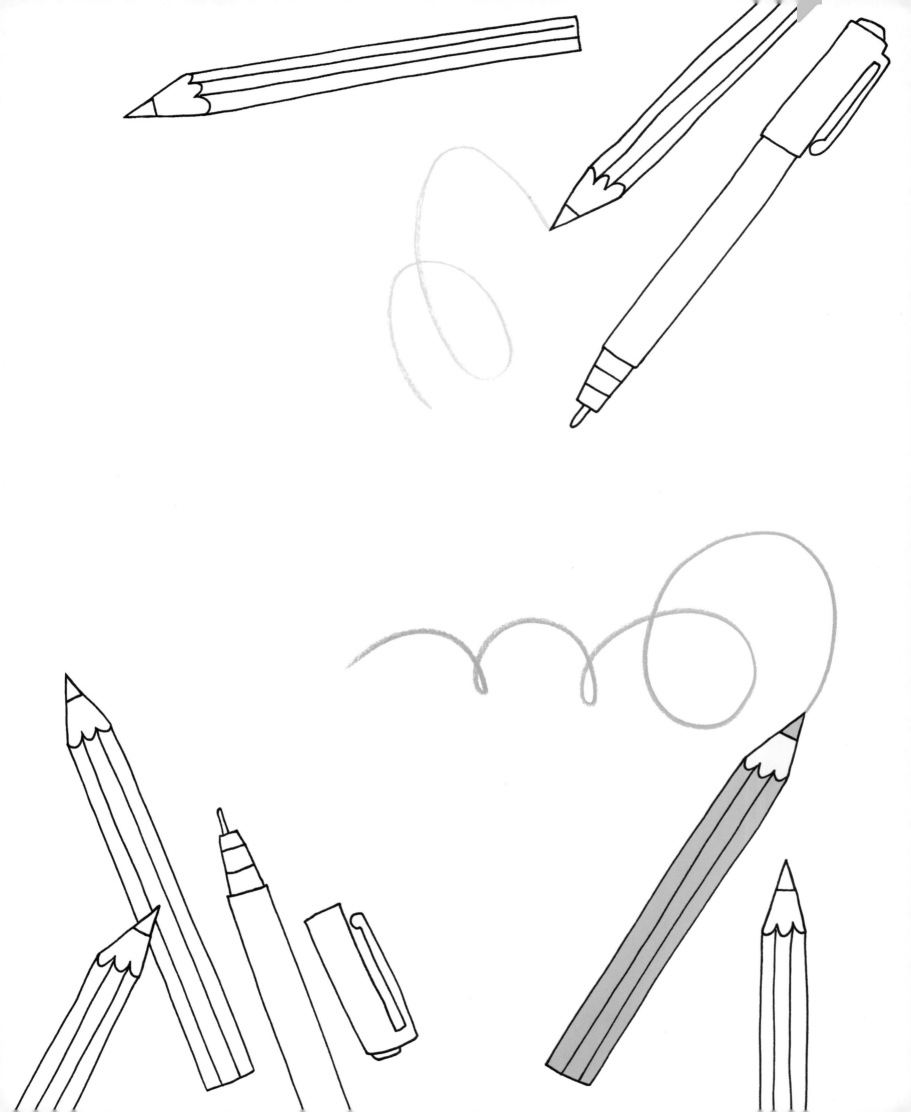

Draw flowers in the empty vases...

...and decorate them, too.

Doodle more frogs...

...and lily pads for them to jump onto.

Fill the shelves with pretty perfume bottles...
or anything else you like.

Doodle flowers, flowers and more flowers.

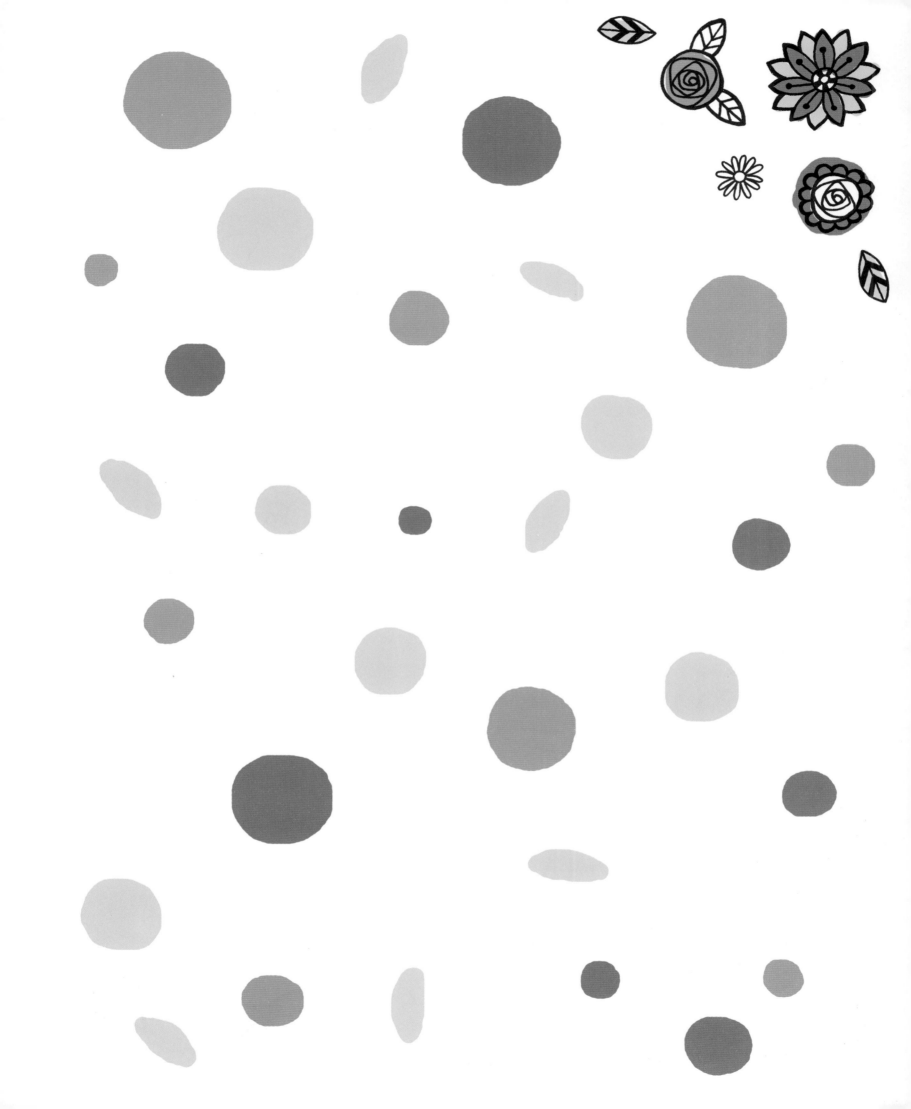

Draw more rabbits...

flowers...

...and crunchy carrots.

Doodle cages for
the songbirds.